GW00722620

IMAGES OF THE
CORNISH COAST

Photographed by John Curtis

SALMON

INTRODUCTION

A county with its own distinctive Celtic heritage, Cornwall has been shaped over centuries by its relationship with the sea. Virtually surrounded by water and with over two hundred and fifty miles of coastline, it is not surprising that fishing has long been Cornwall's most widespread industry, but trade by sea has also played an important part, both for exporting Cornwall's rich natural resources and for importing exotic goods.

A characteristic of the county is the little fishing village or small port, frequently nestling in a steep-sided valley leading down to the sea and with a tiny harbour, often protected by a massive breakwater. The fishing and sea trade has now largely departed but these picturesque communities have managed to retain their distinctive charm and links with their past. Once an isolated part of England, Cornwall became a popular holiday destination as railway and then road transport became more accessible and visitors flocked to enjoy the spectacular scenery, the beautiful beaches and the unhurried way of life. Towns like Newquay and St. Ives developed from little fishing communities into bustling resorts and villages like Looe and Polperro found themselves placed well and truly on the tourist trail.

One of the attractions of Cornwall's coast is its variety. In the west of the county the coastline is rugged and carved into cliffs and offshore rocks by Atlantic storms. Land's End, England's most westerly point, faces out towards America and the small communities that have grown up along this stretch of coast are well used to the unpredictable nature of the sea. Moving east along the coast and into the English Channel, however, the aspect changes and becomes a little more mellow. The Lizard peninsula, with its meandering ancient sunken lanes and tiny hamlets is one of the most beautiful parts of the county, and this in turn leads on to the creeks and little ports of the Helford River, the immense natural harbour at Falmouth and the beautiful Roseland peninsula. From here to the boundary of Cornwall at the River Tamar there are sandy beaches and delightful fishing villages, all set amongst rolling coastal scenery.

The north coast of the county is characterised by its resorts and cliff scenery. To the west are Newquay and St. Ives with their communities of surfers and artists and to the east are Bude and Padstow, a favourite with families for their accessibility to the beautiful beaches of this part of the coast.

As well as its natural beauty, all around the Cornish coast are reminders of the ancient heritage of this county. From the dramatic ruins of King Arthur's Castle at Tintagel, to ruined mine engine houses which often seem to cling precariously to the cliff edge and ancient churches and clifftop chapels, man's attempt to live and work in this beautiful but often unforgiving landscape is everywhere in evidence. Once they may have been unwelcome intrusions on the scene but now they have become an integral part of the landscape itself, beloved by artists and photographers. Whatever the visitor seeks to find from the Cornish coast, be it the cliff scenery, the golden sands and surf, or simply to experience this unique area, they will rarely be disappointed.

ST. IVES
With its fine beaches, picturesque setting and clear light, St. Ives is a favourite with artists and holiday-makers alike. The busy harbour is backed by narrow streets and quaint cottages.

PORTH KIDNEY SANDS
Close to the village of Lelant and facing St. Ives Bay, Porth Kidney Sands are characterised by the huge expanse of sand available at low tide, making it a firm favourite with families.

LEVANT MINE, PENDEEN
With the lighthouse on Pendeen Point in the background, the engine houses at Levant Mine are an evocative reminder that tin mining carried on in Cornwall until the late 20th century.

BOTALLACK MINE
Perched precariously on the cliff edge at Cape Cornwall, the mine workings at Botallack stretch more than a mile out under the sea. The mine was finally closed in 1895.

SENNEN COVE
The nearest safe haven to Land's End, the small harbour at Sennen Cove faces the wide sweep of Whitsand Bay. The Roundhouse once housed a winch to haul boats up the slipway.

LAND'S END

Westernmost point of Cornwall, the cliffs at Land's End face the full force of the Atlantic. Carved into dramatic shapes by storms, the cliffs have been the graveyard of many ships.

LONGSHIPS LIGHTHOUSE

A slender needle visible from Land's End, Longships Lighthouse has warned shipping away from the coast since 1795. Fully automated, the lighthouse is in the care of The Corporation of Trinity House.

LAMORNA COVE

A small breakwater provides protection at Lamorna Cove, on the southern coast of West Cornwall. Set on one of the most spectacular parts of the coast, it is a favourite spot for walkers on the coast path.

MINACK THEATRE

Overlooking the bay at Porthcurno, the Minack Theatre has been staging performances since 1932. Seemingly carved from the solid rock, it was the brainchild of Rowena Cade.

NEWLYN
Its harbour thronged with boats, Newlyn lies on the western side of Mount's Bay. Home to one of the largest fishing fleets in Britain, the Newlyn Fish Festival is held every August.

MOUSEHOLE

The tranquillity of the village of Mousehole belies its history, as it was laid waste by a Spanish raid in 1595. The harbour is the scene each year of spectacular Christmas illuminations.

ST. MICHAEL'S MOUNT
Crowned by its castle, romantic St. Michael's Mount is a rocky pyramid rising out of the waters of Mount's Bay near Marazion. A granite causeway provides a link with the mainland at low tide.

THE LIZARD
With a rugged coastline indented with small coves and fishing villages, and narrow sunken lanes criss-crossing the countryside, the Lizard peninsula possesses some of the most unspoilt scenery in Cornwall.

KYNANCE COVE

With its sandy beach and rugged rock formations, beautiful Kynance Cove, on the western coast of the Lizard, is a favoured spot for artists and photographers. Looking west it enjoys spectacular sunsets.

LIZARD POINT

Most southerly point in Britain, Lizard Point is crowned by its white-painted lighthouse and there has been a light here since 1751. The local dark green serpentine stone was a favourite with the Victorians.

MULLION COVE
The sturdy harbour walls at Mullion Cove, on the Lizard, were built at the end of the 19th century after several seasons of severe storms had decimated the local pilchard industry.

CADGWITH

Fishing boats still go out every day from the little Lizard village of Cadgwith. With its stream following the valley past ancient cottages, it is the epitome of a Cornish fishing village.

CARRICK ROADS

Forming one of the largest natural harbours in the world, Carrick Roads provides safe anchorage for shipping calling at Falmouth or seeking refuge from the storms which can lash this part of the coast.

ST. MAWES

The elegant little resort of St. Mawes lies opposite Falmouth and is a favoured spot with water sports enthusiasts. A sturdy stone castle guards one side of the entrance to Falmouth Harbour.

FALMOUTH
Surrounded by ancient houses and inns, Custom House Quay forms the heart of old Falmouth. Its heritage is celebrated in the National Maritime Museum, but the town still possesses a thriving port.

PORTSCATHO
Set on the eastern side of the Roseland peninsula, the village of Portscatho faces the sweep of Gerrans Bay. This one-time centre for pilchard fishing is now one of the most popular holiday villages in Cornwall.

ST. ANTHONY'S LIGHTHOUSE
Facing out across the busy waters at the entrance to Falmouth Harbour, the lighthouse at St. Anthony Head warns shipping away from the notorious Manacles Rocks, south of the harbour entrance.

ST. JUST-IN-ROSELAND
Perched beside a tidal creek, the 13th century church at St. Just-in-Roseland stands in a beautiful setting amongst semitropical plants and trees. Paths from here lead back to the coast path at St. Mawes.

NARE HEAD

Cared for by The National Trust, the great mass of Nare Head juts out at the eastern end of Gerrans Bay. A favourite walking area, from the 300-foot summit there are sweeping views east and west along the coast.

PORTLOE

Set between steep cliffs, the little harbour at Portloe faces Veryan Bay and once supported a thriving fishing industry. Today, its unspoilt charm is its chief resource, although there is still some lobster and crab potting.

PERRANPORTH

The beautiful three-mile-long beach makes Perranporth the perfect place for surfers and sand yachters. At the southern end of the beach sit the distinctive rock formations known as the Arch and Chapel Rocks.

NEWQUAY

A leading centre for surfing and a busy resort, the little harbour at Newquay is a reminder of its fishing heritage. Houses and hotels nestling among the cliffs, overlook the peaceful scene.

BEDRUTHAN STEPS

Set amidst spectacular coastal scenery, Bedruthan Steps are rocky outcrops which legend has it were a giant's stepping stones. Cared for by The National Trust, clifftop walks give fine views of the rocks below.

CONSTANTINE BAY

Low headlands and rocky islands heading out to sea characterise Constantine Bay. The rock pools, with their abundance of wildlife, and low rich sand dunes all add to the beauty of this sandy cove.

HARLYN BAY

Arguably one of the best beaches in North Cornwall, Harlyn Bay is excellent for surfing and swimming and provides fine walks around the headland. It looks out across the estuary towards Mother Ivey's Bay.

TREVOSE HEAD
Carved out of volcanic rock, rugged Trevose Head is capped by a graceful white painted lighthouse. Either side of the headland are fine sandy beaches at Mother Ivey's Bay and Constantine Bay.

TREVONE
Located between Padstow and Harlyn Bay, Trevone boasts two beaches, one sandy and the other rocky, with a natural swimming pool. A curious feature is a giant 'blow hole' reputedly at least 80 feet deep.

PADSTOW

The waters of the harbour reflect the lights as fishing boats lie at their moorings. Still a busy port, Padstow is one of the most popular centres on the North Cornish coast.

ROCK

The protection of the headland and Braey Hill makes Rock a haven for small boats. Lying opposite Padstow across the Camel Estuary, it is much quieter than its livelier neighbour.

POLZEATH

Benefiting from Atlantic swells and a gradually shelving, sandy beach, Polzeath is one of the finest surfing resorts in Cornwall. To the delight of visitors, dolphins and seals make regular surfing companions.

CAMEL ESTUARY

With its inlets and sandy beaches the Camel Estuary has long been a favourite centre for family holidays. It is sheltered to the north by the bulk of Pentire Point and encompasses the busy resorts of Polzeath and Padstow.

PORT ISAAC

A charming fishing village, Port Isaac nestles in a narrow sheltered valley. The dramatic setting under high, rocky cliffs and its character give the village a timeless feel.

PORT QUIN

Port Quin is today a tranquil cove apparently hardly touched by the modern world. It achieved some fame when used as a setting for the popular TV series 'Poldark', based on Winston Graham's books of the same name.

TINTAGEL
The birthplace of the legendary King Arthur, Tintagel lies on a dramatic stretch of coast.
The ruined castle stands on a rocky headland with Merlin's Cave on the beach below.

BOSCASTLE
Leading inland to the Valency Valley, the harbour at Boscastle lies hidden from the sea behind massive headlands. The Lookout above the harbour, offers fine views of the coast.

THE STRANGLES

North of Boscastle is High Cliff, the highest point on the coast of Cornwall. From here there are striking views of The Strangles, famous for its black pebbles with quartz streaks.

MORWENSTOW
A wild outpost of high cliffs, wooded valleys and rolling farmland, Morwenstow is known for its association with Rev. R. S. Hawker, who devised the tradition of Harvest Festival.

MEVAGISSEY
Named after Saints Meva and Issey, the fishing village and resort of Mevagissey lies south of St. Austell. Narrow streets of fishermen's houses cluster behind the busy harbour.

GRIBBEN HEAD
Jutting out into the sea at the eastern end of the St. Austell Bay, Gribben Head is capped by an 84-feet-high beacon erected in 1832, at the entrance to the Fowey Estuary.

FOWEY

Set on a hillside overlooking the estuary, the old streets in Fowey reveal views of the river below. Opposite, across the estuary, lies the village of Polruan, once a centre for boat building.

PAR SANDS

Facing the sweep of St. Austell Bay, Par Sands is a large sandy beach, bordered by sand dunes. It is only three miles from the famous Eden Project, a living theatre of plants and people, opened in 2001.

LANTIC BAY

A quiet, beautiful bay with white sands, Lantic Bay is situated to the east of Polruan. Viewed here from Pencarrow Head, it is best reached by boat, being fairly inaccessible on foot.

POLPERRO

Packed tightly into a steep valley, Polperro is one of the prettiest villages in Cornwall. The busy harbour is backed by narrow lanes of picturesque old fishermen's cottages.

TALLAND
On the south coast of Cornwall facing Talland Bay, between Polperro and Looe, Talland is a tiny hamlet comprised of an ancient church, vicarage and a handful of cottages.

LOOE ISLAND

Lying about a mile off the coast near the mouth of the River Looe, legend has it that Looe Island was once visited by Joseph of Arimathea.

RAME HEAD

The Rame peninsula, in the extreme south-east of Cornwall, has been designated an Area of Outstanding Natural Beauty. At Rame Head, its most southern point, stands the ancient Chapel of St. Michael.

Published by J. Salmon Ltd., Sevenoaks, Kent TN13 1BB. © 2009
Website: www.jsalmon.co.uk. Telephone: 01732 452381. Email: enquiries@jsalmon.co.uk.

Design and photographs by John Curtis © John Curtis.

With special thanks to Philip Jackson at the Minack Theatre, John McMurray and Rob Yeomans.

ISBN 978-1-84640-182-4

Title page photograph: Cliffs at Tintagel Half title page photograph: Low tide in St. Ives Harbour
Front cover photograph: Bedruthan Steps Back cover photograph: St. Mawes

Salmon Books

ENGLISH IMAGES SERIES

Photography by John Curtis

Titles available in this series